D0970260

Now You're a Graduate

written and compiled by
Ellyn Sanna

BARBOUR
PUBLISHING, INC.

$\mathcal{N}$ow that you're a graduate, many challenges lie ahead. I'm proud of all you have accomplished in the past years—and I pray now that you'll continue to excel in the years that come. May you. . .

🎓 make wise choices.

🎓 have the courage and determination to act in the present, rather than procrastinating.

🎓 follow your dreams.

🎓 most of all, always put your trust in God.

A Time to Choose

Reject the wrong and choose the right.

ISAIAH 7:15

*Every time you make a choice you are turning
the central part of you, the part that chooses,
into something a little different than what it was before.*

C. S. LEWIS

*L*ife will offer you many choices.
My prayer for you is that God will grant you the strength
and wisdom to always choose wisely.

*God asks no one whether he will accept life.
That is not the choice.
You must take it.
The only choice is how.*

HENRY WARD BEECHER

We find in life exactly what we put into it.

RALPH WALDO EMERSON

Choose your life with thought and consideration. Don't let your life be something that happens to you while you're doing something else. Decide what you want to put into life; think about what you want to find in the years ahead. . .and then make the choices that will take you there. If you want a life that includes a successful career, then work hard. If you want a life that makes a difference, that changes the world for the better, then get involved. If you want a life that's filled with love and friendships and family, then be loving and caring and supportive in all your relationships. Commit yourself to doing the best job you can at whatever you do.

Vince Lombardi, former coach of the Green Bay Packers, said, "The quality of a person's life is in direct proportion to their commitment to excellence, regardless of their chosen field of endeavor." It's not luck that gives you a good life. You get to choose. Are you committed to quality?

FAITH STEWART

*Character building begins in
our infancy and continues until our death.*

ELEANOR ROOSEVELT

*Y*ou have a good start in life. But this isn't the end. In fact, your graduation is a whole new beginning. The person you will be ten years from now—or fifty—depends on the choices you make in the next few years. Don't make these decisions lightly.

I pray that God will guide you.

One falsehood spoils a thousand truths.

AFRICAN PROVERB

$\mathcal{M}$ay you always choose the truth.

That's not always as easy as it sounds. It's so easy to tell lies. Sometimes they slip out of our mouths before we even think. Not big lies, usually, just little untruths. They don't seem very important. After all, everyone tells a lie or two. You almost have to lie occasionally just to navigate some social situations.

But don't you believe it. Just because our world accepts that lying is a part of life doesn't mean that you have to as well. Be a person of integrity. Stand up for the truth.

Speaking the truth in love,
we will in all things grow up into him who is the Head,
that is, Christ.

EPHESIANS 4:15

Some people try to avoid making choices at all. They don't want to make the wrong choice—and the consequences of even the right choice can be frightening. And so they try to walk the fence. They think that way no one can accuse them of anything.

But remember Pilate. He knew Jesus was innocent. But Pilate didn't have the courage to choose to do the right thing. He washed his hands of making a decision. And Jesus went to His death.

I pray that you will never be afraid to take a stand. Stand up for right. Make your choice known.

All that is essential for the triumph of evil is that good men do nothing.

EDMUND BURKE

To every man there openeth
A Way, and Ways, and a Way,
And the High Soul climbs the High Way,
And the Low Soul gropes the Low,
And in between, on the misty flats,
The rest drift to and fro.
But to every man there openeth
A High Way, and a Low.
And every man decideth
The way his soul shall go.

JOHN OXENHAM

There is a way that seems right to a man,
but in the end it leads to death.
. . .The fear of the Lord is a fountain of life,
turning a man from the snares of death.

PROVERBS 14:12, 27

Choose for yourselves this day whom you will serve. . . .
But as for me. . .[I] will serve the Lord.

JOSHUA 24:15

How much better to get wisdom than gold,
to choose understanding rather than silver!

PROVERBS 16:16

Use It or Lose It

Who will be able to run a five-minute mile,
slam dunk a dozen shots,
bench press four hundred pounds,
or captain a winning team. . .
ten years from now?
Use it or lose it

Who will be able to play the trumpet,
write poetry,
paint with acrylics,
or act on stage. . .
twenty years from now?
Use it or lose it.

Who will be able to utilize grammar's finer rules,
algebra's tedious equations,
history's dates and places,
or chemistry's volatile reactions. . .
thirty years from now?
Use it or lose it.

Who will be able to manage money wisely,
innovating useful products,
investing in others,
or helping the poor. . .
forty years from now?
Use it or lose it.

Who will be able to hear God's commendation for
serving faithfully,
loving passionately,
and being all you were created to be. . .
fifty years from now?
Use it or lose it.

No one can excel in everything.
The decades demand decisions.
Choose wisely.
Your choices pinpoint your priorities
and determine your destiny.
Use it or lose it.

PATRICIA SOUDER

Only God can satisfy the hungry heart.

HUGH BLACK

*I*n the past, you may have accepted your parents' decisions for your life. If they went to church, you went to church. If they called themselves Christians, you went along with their beliefs.

But now it's time to choose for yourself.

DO YOU CHOOSE CHRIST?

I find the great thing in this world is not so much where we stand as in what direction we are moving.

OLIVER WENDELL HOLMES

Do It Now!

Today, if you hear his voice,
do not harden your hearts. . . .

PSALM 95:7-8

*A*void the dangers of procrastination. Almost everyone has good intentions—but not all of us get around to putting those intentions into action.

Don't put off until tomorrow the action God's nudging you to take today.

DO IT NOW!

> *Wisdom is knowing what to do next.*
> *Skill is knowing how to do it.*
> *Virtue is doing it.*
>
> THOMAS JEFFERSON

Let him who would move the world first move himself.

SENECA

Don't put off for tomorrow what you can do today,
because if you enjoy it today,
you can do it again tomorrow.

JAMES A. MICHENER

Luck is a matter of preparation meeting opportunity.

OPRAH WINFREY

If you've got a job to do,
Do it now!
If you're sure the job's your own,
Do not hem and haw and groan—
Do it now!
Don't put off a bit of work,
Do it now!
It doesn't pay to shirk,
Do it now!

MARY DAWSON HUGHES

The beginning is the most important part of the work.

PLATO

*P*erhaps the most valuable result of all education is
the ability to make oneself do the thing you have to do,
whether you like it or not.
This is the first lesson to be learned.

THOMAS HENRY HUXLEY

I am only one, but I am still one;
I cannot do everything,
but I can still do something;
and because I cannot do everything
I will not refuse to do the something that I can do.

EDWARD EVERETT HALE

Sooner or later in the years to come, you'll look around and realize you've taken a wrong turn somewhere along the line. Instead of turning around immediately, however, you'll be tempted to keep going. After all, you've invested a lot of time and effort in that particular course of action. If you change course now, your friends and family may think you're being irresponsible. Or you may have to admit that they were right when they advised you not to take this road in the first place. Pride alone may keep you heading along your misguided way.

But when you realize you're on the wrong track, don't waste any more time. Who cares if you look foolish? If your road won't take you where you want to go, what's the point in following it any longer? Turn around at once.

It's never too late to begin again.

No matter how far you have gone on the wrong road, turn back.

TURKISH PROVERB

*It is the greatest of all mistakes to do nothing
because you can only do a little.
Do what you can.*

SYDNEY SMITH

Sometimes the size of the job will keep you from acting. Like David looking up at Goliath, you'll feel too little to fight the giant that looms over you. After all, the odds are clearly against you. What's the point of even trying?

When those thoughts threaten to stop you in your tracks, remember—David didn't let Goliath's size stop him. Instead, he picked up his little pebble and killed a giant.

Do what you can, with what you have, where you are.

THEODORE ROOSEVELT

Don't Be Afraid to Dream

Slowly, steadily, surely,
the time approaches when the vision will be fulfilled.
If it seems slow, wait patiently, for it will surely take place.
It will not be delayed.

HABAKKUK 2:3 NLT

Everything that is done in this world is done by hope.

MARTIN LUTHER

Life is either a daring adventure or nothing.

HELEN KELLER

*All our dreams can come true if
we have the courage to pursue them.*

WALT DISNEY

As you look toward the future, don't be afraid to dream. God will use your dreams if you give them to Him. Dare to dream big dreams and then wait on God. You may be surprised what He will do.

With man this impossible,
but with God all things are possible.

MATTHEW 19:26

$\mathcal{D}$id you hear about the little mouse who hitched a ride across a bridge on the back of a huge elephant? When they got to the other side, the mouse said, "Whew! Did you see how we made that bridge shake?"

Deep down inside, you, too, want to shake your world—but you have sense enough to know you're no elephant.

Don't worry. God doesn't expect you to be. In Ephesians 1:19 NLT, Paul says, "I pray that you will begin to understand the incredible greatness of his power for us who believe him."

So hop on board. With God, you can make a difference. For eternity!

PATRICIA SOUDER

I dream for a living.

Steven Spielberg

The poor man is not he who is without a cent
but he who is without a dream.

Harry Kemp

*Courage is the power of being
mastered and possessed with an idea.*

Phillips Brooks

Keep thou thy dreams—
The tissue of all wings
Is woven first of them;
From dreams are made
The precious and imperishable things,
Whose loveliness lives on and does not fade.

VIRNA SHEAD

Young People Are Like Kites

You spend a lifetime trying to get them off the ground.
You run with them until you're breathless. . .they crash.
You add a longer tail. . .they hit the rooftop.
You pluck them out of the spout.
You patch and comfort, adjust and teach.
You watch them lifted by the wind
and assure them that someday they'll fly.
Finally, they're airborne, but they need more string,
and you keep letting it out,
and with each twist of the ball of twine,
there is a sadness that goes with the joy
because the kite becomes more distant.

And somehow you know that it won't be long
before that beautiful creature
will snap the lifeline that bound you together
and soar as it was meant to soar. . .free and alone.
Only then do you know you did your job.

AUTHOR UNKNOWN

𝒴ou have a story, a story that you're living. So far, you've only lived the first few chapters. Much of what your story contains has been decided by the people in your life. You didn't get to choose your family or where you would live or other aspects of your life. But now you get to write the rest of your story; you get to choose what to do with what you've been given so far. It's kind of like one of those "choose your own adventure" books. And you will have adventures.

But choose carefully and wisely. . .and don't be afraid to follow your dreams. When you do, you, too, will soar like a kite. With a prayer in our hearts, we older folks will step back and watch you fly.

FAITH STEWART

*W*e grow great by dreams.
All big men are dreamers.
They see things in the soft haze of
a spring day or in the red fire of a long winter's evening.
Some of us let these great dreams die,
but others nourish and protect them,
nurse them through bad days till they bring
them to the sunshine and light which
come always to those who sincerely hope
that their dreams will come true.

WOODROW WILSON

Trust God

It is better to take refuge in the Lord
than to trust in man.

PSALM 118:8

*Y*ou have many talents, numerous strengths. These are God's good gifts to you. But my prayer for you is that you will never put your strength in these things. . .nor in anything else, whether money or possessions or recognition or achievement. May you rely only on the strength of God in all you do.

When you do, you will find true success in life.

Four things a man must learn to do
If he would keep his record true:
To think, without confusion, clearly. . .
To love his fellow man sincerely. . .
To act from motives purely. . .
To trust in God and Heaven securely.

HENRY VAN DYKE

On the Threshold of Time

*L*ord Jesus, as we look into the future, let no fears assail us. Help us to be confident that Thou wilt be with us in the future as we know Thou hast been in the past.

We know that our Christianity is no insurance policy against trouble, but rather the guarantee that Thou wilt be with us in the trouble. That should give us strong hearts and confident faith. For so long as Thou art beside us, loving us, helping us, what have we to fear?

Hear us as we pray, standing on the threshold of time. Thou alone can equip us for the tasks and duties that are ours, that we may do our very best. . . .

PETER MARSHALL

As you graduate, odds are you're getting ready to leave home as well. In my office I have a poster that says "Home is where you start from." It shows a little boy setting off for his first day of school. His hair is combed, his clothes are brand new. Standing in the doorway, sending him on his way, are his parents. Dozens of hearts tumble out around them, representing the love that follows the little boy.

Love follows you as well. But breaking away from your home can be scary. Sometimes it hurts. But if you don't leave the old behind, you'll never grasp the new gifts God has in store for you. Your home and all its love will always be there for you; when you let go of the past and move on to something different, you don't lose what you had; you merely gain something more.

REMEMBER: If a caterpillar refused to change, it could never become a butterfly. Trust God to give you wings.

FAITH STEWART

Be like the bird
That, pausing in her flight
Awhile on boughs too slight,
Feels them give way
Beneath her and yet sings,
Knowing that she hath wings.

VICTOR HUGO

The way to God has properly been described as "letting oneself fall," and has been compared with the first flight of a baby eagle, pushed out of the nest by its parents, and then discovering to its amazement that the invisible ocean of light in which it is dropping is capable of bearing it up. The presence of God which surrounds everyone is like this invisible ocean which bears us up more surely than do all visible means of security.

KARL HEIM

May you have the courage to
let yourself drop
into the hands of God.

God is always at work.
Believe this not only when you
bask in the sun and feast on God's blessings
but also when you struggle with
the storms of life and fear destruction.
God is always at work.
Believe this not only when you win your race and receive awards
but also when you come in last and feel defeated.
God is always at work.
Believe this and do what is right
even when others don't understand. . .
and you don't understand why they don't understand.
God is always at work.
Believe this when you don't see what He is doing.
Noah had never seen rain when he built the ark.
Abraham and Sarah had no idea where they were going
when they left for the Promised Land.
Moses and Ruth, Daniel and Esther. . .
and millions of others succeeded in life
because they believed and acted on this truth:
God is always at work.

PATRICIA SOUDER

Graduate's Prayer

On this graduation day, Lord, help me to remember all that I have learned. I know this is not the end of my learning process but a new beginning. Keep me open to Your leading; may I recognize Your path for my life. Remind me that I am created in Your image; I know I am Your child.

When I stumble, steady me. Make me strong and guide me with Your love. Remind me I am never alone. Teach me to recognize Your presence in times of stress and anxiety; convinced that You are by my side.

Help me be the person You want me to be as I go forth to serve on this my graduation day.

MARY HERRON